How to Be the Man of Your Wife's Dreams . . . and not her worst nightmare!

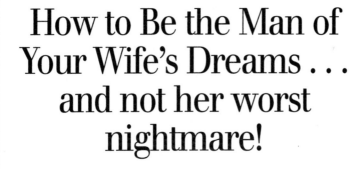

Introduction

How To Be The Man of Your Wife's Dreams . . . and not her worst nightmare! is a delightfully amusing combination of truth and jest. Filled with quotes which alternately poke fun at and lend tremendous insight into everyday married life, this clever little pocketbook will bring a chuckle and perhaps a playful wince now and then to men and women alike.

These quotes will entertain couples who have been married for years, those recently engaged or married, and singles who ever entertained the thought! Overflowing with both wit and wisdom, *How To Be The Man of Your Wife's Dreams . . . and not her worst nightmare!* will be the perfect gift for Valentine's Day, your best friends' wedding showers and anniversaries, and all around special occasions.

This little pocketbook of quotes will encourage you to both laugh and learn! Be sure to put this humorous keepsake on your coffee table for interesting conversation and table talk, then give one to a friend to bring a ray of light-hearted sunshine into another life.

And don't forget to pick up a copy of its companion pocketbook *How To Be The Woman of Your Husband's Dreams . . . and not his worst nightmare!* Then sit back, laugh, and have a jolly good time!

Take her out
for a romantic
candlelight dinner.

HOW TO BE THE MAN OF YOUR WIFE'S DREAMS

Ask her to pay for the meal.

AND NOT HER WORST NIGHTMARE

Tell her how much you love her cooking!

Slip her one of your
mom's recipes.

AND NOT HER WORST NIGHTMARE

Show her you love her
by working hard.

Show her who's boss
by working her hard.

AND NOT HER WORST NIGHTMARE

When a boorish
jerk insults her,
stand up for her.

HOW TO BE THE MAN OF YOUR WIFE'S DREAMS

Stand there and
say nothing.

AND NOT HER WORST NIGHTMARE

When she's afraid
and needs you to comfort
her, assure her you
are there for her no
matter what happens.

HOW TO BE THE MAN OF YOUR WIFE'S DREAMS

Tell her to go watch
a good movie —
"A good Three Stooges
comedy always does
the trick for me."

AND NOT HER WORST NIGHTMARE

Compliment her
on the way she
runs the house.

HOW TO BE THE MAN OF YOUR WIFE'S DREAMS

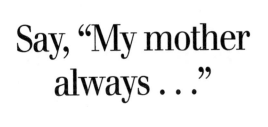

Say, "My mother always . . ."

AND NOT HER WORST NIGHTMARE

Surprise her
by helping with
the housework.

HOW TO BE THE MAN OF YOUR WIFE'S DREAMS

When she catches you rebuilding that smelly carburetor in the living room, say "Surprise!"

AND NOT HER WORST NIGHTMARE

Gaze into her eyes.

HOW TO BE THE MAN OF YOUR WIFE'S DREAMS

Gape at her thighs.

AND NOT HER WORST NIGHTMARE

Tell her you want to grow old with her.

HOW TO BE THE MAN OF YOUR WIFE'S DREAMS

Point out the "Oil of Olay" on your next trip to the store together.

AND NOT HER WORST NIGHTMARE

Make it a priority
to follow through
on your promises.

HOW TO BE THE MAN OF YOUR WIFE'S DREAMS

Make it a priority
to follow through
on your golf swing.

Whisper sweet nothings in her ear.

HOW TO BE THE MAN OF YOUR WIFE'S DREAMS

Give her a Wet Willy!

AND NOT HER WORST NIGHTMARE.

Make breakfast
and serve it to
her in bed.

Demand she
make breakfast
and the bed!

AND NOT HER WORST NIGHTMARE

When she needs you
most, be a sweetheart
and hold her tight.

HOW TO BE THE MAN OF YOUR WIFE'S DREAMS

When she needs you most, be a louse and put her down.

AND NOT HER WORST NIGHTMARE

Light her fire with a kiss and candlelight.

HOW TO BE THE MAN OF YOUR WIFE'S DREAMS

Tell her to turn on the lights and complain, "What's the deal with all the candles?"

AND NOT HER WORST NIGHTMARE

Admire her
handmade crafts.

HOW TO BE THE MAN OF YOUR WIFE'S DREAMS

Ask her what trash can she found them in.

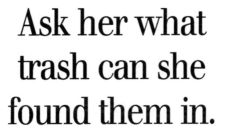

AND NOT HER WORST NIGHTMARE

Tell her what a "great love" yours is.

HOW TO BE THE MAN OF YOUR WIFE'S DREAMS

Remind her what a "great lover" you are.

AND NOT HER WORST NIGHTMARE

Bring her fresh-cut flowers.

HOW TO BE THE MAN OF YOUR WIFE'S DREAMS

Remind her to weed the flower bed.

AND NOT HER WORST NIGHTMARE

Give her your undivided
time and attention
at least one evening
per week.

Refuse to give her
the time of day every
day of the week.

AND NOT HER WORST NIGHTMARE

Allow her to plan
the decor and
decorate the home.

HOW TO BE THE MAN OF YOUR WIFE'S DREAMS

Insist on hanging
your Woodstock
poster in the den.

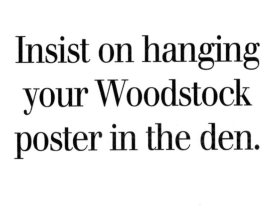

AND NOT HER WORST NIGHTMARE

41

Look her in the
eyes when she's
talking to you.

42

HOW TO BE THE MAN OF YOUR WIFE'S DREAMS

When she's trying
to talk to you,
keep glancing
at the television.

AND NOT HER WORST NIGHTMARE

Shower, shave,
and put on cologne
just for her.

HOW TO BE THE MAN OF YOUR WIFE'S DREAMS

Don't take a shower, shave, or brush your teeth. Then tell her you want a big kiss.

AND NOT HER WORST NIGHTMARE

Gently rub her neck
and shoulders to
soothe her at the end
of a long, stressful day.

HOW TO BE THE MAN OF YOUR WIFE'S DREAMS

Surprise her from behind, bury your chin in her neck, and scrape her with your whiskers.

AND NOT HER WORST NIGHTMARE

Surprise her with
two front-row tickets
to Julio Iglesias.

HOW TO BE THE MAN OF YOUR WIFE'S DREAMS

Take her on
a surprise date to
the tractor pulls.

AND NOT HER WORST NIGHTMARE

Kiss her fingers and the back of her hand.

Slap her on the
back as you
pass by.

AND NOT HER WORST NIGHTMARE

Clean up the kitchen when it's messy. Mess up the kitchen when it's clean. Softly sing *You're So Beautiful to Me* into her answering machine so she'll get it during the middle of the afternoon.

Call her up in the afternoon and if she's not there say, "Are you shopping *again*?" on the answering machine.

AND NOT HER WORST NIGHTMARE

Pick up a book by her
favorite author, and
surprise her with it.

HOW TO BE THE MAN OF YOUR WIFE'S DREAMS

Tell her she has too much housework to waste time reading.

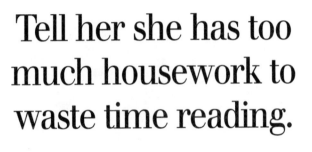

55

Tell her how
good she looks
in her new outfit.

HOW TO BE THE MAN OF YOUR WIFE'S DREAMS

Ask her, "Isn't that
outfit a little young
for you?"

57

AND NOT HER WORST NIGHTMARE

Rub her feet
while you talk.

HOW TO BE THE MAN OF YOUR WIFE'S DREAMS

Just as she is telling you how much you mean to her, say, "What smells?"

AND NOT HER WORST NIGHTMARE

When she gains
a little weight,
overlook it.

HOW TO BE THE MAN OF YOUR WIFE'S DREAMS

Put one of those pigs
that snort in the
refrigerator as
a subtle hint.

Turn on soft
music and turn
down the light.

HOW TO BE THE MAN OF YOUR WIFE'S DREAMS

Turn on talk radio.

AND NOT HER WORST NIGHTMARE

Sit quietly beside
her on the couch.

HOW TO BE THE MAN OF YOUR WIFE'S DREAMS

Say, "Get up, will ya'?
I want to stretch out."

AND NOT HER WORST NIGHTMARE

When she smiles
at you in a crowd,
smile back.

Act like you
didn't notice.

AND NOT HER WORST NIGHTMARE

Serenade her
with some of her
favorite "oldies."

HOW TO BE THE MAN OF YOUR WIFE'S DREAMS

Read to her the latest financials from *The Wall Street Journal.*

AND NOT HER WORST NIGHTMARE

Tell her you
missed her while
you were fishing.

HOW TO BE THE MAN OF YOUR WIFE'S DREAMS

Tell her you plan
to fish every weekend
you get the chance.

AND NOT HER WORST NIGHTMARE

Tell her your favorite
thing in the world is
spending time with her.

HOW TO BE THE MAN OF YOUR WIFE'S DREAMS

Tell her how much you enjoy the freedom of your frequent business trips.

AND NOT HER WORST NIGHTMARE

Place her picture
on your desk where
everyone can see it.

HOW TO BE THE MAN OF YOUR WIFE'S DREAMS

Place a picture of
you and your
favorite hunting dog
on your desk.

AND NOT HER WORST NIGHTMARE

Kiss her lips and look into her eyes while you tell her about your day.

HOW TO BE THE MAN OF YOUR WIFE'S DREAMS

When she asks
about your day, pick
up the newspaper
and grunt, "Okay."

AND NOT HER WORST NIGHTMARE

Let her know you are madly in love with her.

HOW TO BE THE MAN OF YOUR WIFE'S DREAMS

Remind her daily
that she makes
you mad.

AND NOT HER WORST NIGHTMARE

Snuggle and make
the first several minutes
of her day warm
and wonderful.

HOW TO BE THE MAN OF YOUR WIFE'S DREAMS

Throw the covers
off of her and
demand she get up
to take out the dog.

AND NOT HER WORST NIGHTMARE

Smile at her and
give her a hug first
thing when you
come in from work.

Ask her what's
for dinner and
why it isn't ready.

AND NOT HER WORST NIGHTMARE

83

Kiss her eyelids
and run your fingers
through her hair.

Pat her on the head
and ask, "When was
the last time you
shaved your legs?"

AND NOT HER WORST NIGHTMARE

Surprise her with
a reservation for
Friday night at
a first-class hotel.

HOW TO BE THE MAN OF YOUR WIFE'S DREAMS

Invite the boys over to watch Monday night football — again!

AND NOT HER WORST NIGHTMARE

Pray with her
over the things
that concern her.

HOW TO BE THE MAN OF YOUR WIFE'S DREAMS

Tell her to take
it up with a shrink.

AND NOT HER WORST NIGHTMARE

First thing after getting
home from work, fix her
a cold drink and ask
her how her day went.

HOW TO BE THE MAN OF YOUR WIFE'S DREAMS

First thing home from work, kick off your shoes, plop down on the couch with the remote and ask her for a cold drink.

AND NOT HER WORST NIGHTMARE

Call her on Wednesday
to ask her for a date
on Friday night to the
restaurant of her choice.

Walk in the door at 6:30 Friday night and say, "Oh, I thought if you were ready, we'd go out . . . but you're not."

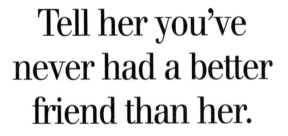

Tell her you've never had a better friend than her.

HOW TO BE THE MAN OF YOUR WIFE'S DREAMS

Tell her you've never had a better friend than your sister Sue.

AND NOT HER WORST NIGHTMARE

Tell her you'd love to spend time with her helping out at the homeless shelter.

HOW TO BE THE MAN OF YOUR WIFE'S DREAMS

Tell her if she
wants a night out
to go help out at the
homeless shelter.

AND NOT HER WORST NIGHTMARE

Plan to get home before
she arrives home from work;
surprise her with a hot
bubble bath, lighted candles,
and her favorite cold drink.
Have the evening catered.

HOW TO BE THE MAN OF YOUR WIFE'S DREAMS

Demand she always
be home before you
with dinner on the table.
Then call an hour late,
and say you're having
dinner with the guys.

AND NOTHER WORST NIGHTMARE

When she makes
a mistake, kiss
her on the nose
and hug her.

HOW TO BE THE MAN OF YOUR WIFE'S DREAMS

When she makes
a mistake, look down
at her, shake your
head back and forth,
and roll your eyes.

AND NOT HER WORST NIGHTMARE

While she is cooking dinner, put on one of her favorite CD's for her to cook by.

HOW TO BE THE MAN OF YOUR WIFE'S DREAMS

When she is preparing the meal, tune into the sports channel and holler frequently, "Is it ready yet?"

AND NOT HER WORST NIGHTMARE

Ask her opinion
about something
that matters to you.

Ask her opinion,
then tell her that what
she said was stupid.

AND NOT HER WORST NIGHTMARE

Take her in your arms and dance with her to soft music.

HOW TO BE THE MAN OF YOUR WIFE'S DREAMS

While you're dancing,
tell her she needs a
breath mint.

AND NOT HER WORST NIGHTMARE

Open the door for her as she gets into the car.

HOW TO BE THE MAN OF YOUR WIFE'S DREAMS

Honk the horn and yell at her to hurry up and get in!

AND NOT HER WORST NIGHTMARE

Mow the lawn and empty the garbage without being asked.

HOW TO BE THE MAN OF YOUR WIFE'S DREAMS

Call her from the office and remind her that the garbage goes today and that you filled the mower with gas.

AND NOT HER WORST NIGHTMARE

One day when she doesn't have make-up on, say, "I love my beautiful wife!"

HOW TO BE THE MAN OF YOUR WIFE'S DREAMS

Walk past her when she is not fixed up and ask, "What happened to your face?"

AND NOT HER WORST NIGHTMARE

When she wants to
talk about her feelings,
sit down right then, take
her hands, look her in the
eyes, and assure her she
can tell you anything.

HOW TO BE THE MAN OF YOUR WIFE'S DREAMS

When she says she wants to talk about her feelings ask her, "Why do you have to be so emotional all the time?"

AND NOT HER WORST NIGHTMARE

When she tries to tell you about a bad habit you have developed, assure her you will work on it.

HOW TO BE THE MAN OF YOUR WIFE'S DREAMS

Bristle and retort: "Nobody's perfect!"

Go for a drive with her on Sunday afternoon, look at the Parade of Homes in the new area of town, and dream about your goals and life together.

HOW TO BE THE MAN OF YOUR WIFE'S DREAMS

When she asks you to go with her to look at the Parade of Homes, tell her to quit pressuring you, that you can't afford that nonsense, then pack up your new bass boat and go fishing.

AND NOT HER WORST NIGHTMARE

Call her during a busy day at work just to tell her you miss her and can't wait to get home to be with her.

HOW TO BE THE MAN OF YOUR WIFE'S DREAMS

When she calls you,
put her on hold.

AND NOT HER WORST NIGHTMARE

Open a savings account
to build up enough
money to surprise
her with tickets for
a three-day cruise.

HOW TO BE THE MAN OF YOUR WIFE'S DREAMS

Tell her if she
wants to get away,
to get a second job.

123

A week before her birthday, tell her you are planning a special celebration just for the two of you. Follow through.

HOW TO BE THE MAN OF YOUR WIFE'S DREAMS

Come up with some really convincing excuses why you didn't even get her a card, such as being busy at work, your boss has been a jerk lately, you don't have time for such nonsense, or what does it matter anyway—it's only a card.

AND NOT HER WORST NIGHTMARE

Offer to buy the
groceries for her,
then put them away.

HOW TO BE THE MAN OF YOUR WIFE'S DREAMS

Tell her she can go to the grocery store while you're playing golf.

AND NOT HER WORST NIGHTMARE

When driving a long
distance together, stop
when she needs to
take a break.

HOW TO BE THE MAN OF YOUR WIFE'S DREAMS

Tell her she has
five minutes and then
it's her turn to drive.

AND NOT HER WORST NIGHTMARE

Spoon feed her chocolate mousse.

'Tell her if she'd snack on raw carrots she could drop ten pounds.

AND NOT HER WORST NIGHTMARE

Ask her to snuggle up next to you in bed and hold her until she falls asleep.

HOW TO BE THE MAN OF YOUR WIFE'S DREAMS

When she gets into
bed, roll over and
pretend you're asleep.

AND NOTHER WORST NIGHTMARE

Gaze at her until
she asks you what
you're looking at.
Then smile and say,
"The most gorgeous
creature on earth."

HOW TO BE THE MAN OF YOUR WIFE'S DREAMS

Bellow at her that she reminds you of the fat lady in the circus.

AND NOT HER WORST NIGHTMARE

Take her to a romantic movie. Sit in the back row, and pull her close and kiss her.

HOW TO BE THE MAN OF YOUR WIFE'S DREAMS

Take her to a professional wrestling match, sit on the front row, and say, "Isn't this a great way to spend the evening?"

AND NOT HER WORST NIGHTMARE

Tell her that her
complexion reminds
you of fine porcelain.

Ask her if she thinks
that big blemish is
going to scar her face
like the last one did.

AND NOT HER WORST NIGHTMARE

Tell her that her lips
remind you of roses.

HOW TO BE THE MAN OF YOUR WIFE'S DREAMS

Bring her home
chapstick, and ask
her to use it.

When she tells you
her feet feel cold,
put them between
your hands and blow
on them to warm them.

HOW TO BE THE MAN OF YOUR WIFE'S DREAMS

Tell her the socks are in the bottom dresser drawer on the right.

AND NOT HER WORST NIGHTMARE

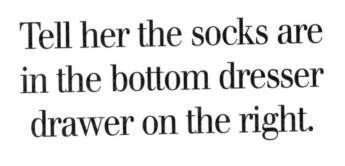

143

Reinforce how smart she is.

HOW TO BE THE MAN OF YOUR WIFE'S DREAMS

Remind her what a
genius you are.

AND NOT HER WORST NIGHTMARE

145

Tell her how much you appreciate the things she does to take pressure off of you.

HOW TO BE THE MAN OF YOUR WIFE'S DREAMS

Tell her not to nag
so much! That it
would take a lot of
pressure off of you.

AND NOT HER WORST NIGHTMARE

Hug her tight.

If she requests a hug, hold her for two seconds, then pull away and give her a pat on the back.

AND NOT HER WORST NIGHTMARE

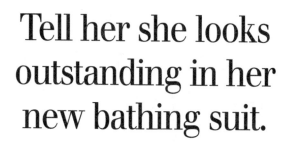

Tell her she looks outstanding in her new bathing suit.

HOW TO BE THE MAN OF YOUR WIFE'S DREAMS

Throw her a towel
and tell her to
please cover up.

AND NOT HER WORST NIGHTMARE

On Valentine's Day bring her a box of fine chocolates.

Give her a toaster.

153

AND NOT HER WORST NIGHTMARE

Ask her to go for a leisurely walk around the neighborhood. Halfway home, stop her in the middle of the street and give her a romantic kiss.

HOW TO BE THE MAN OF YOUR WIFE'S DREAMS

Halfway home, mutter, "You are *so* out of shape!"

AND NOT HER WORST NIGHTMARE